Old Harrogate
Paul Chrystal

Harrogate featured in the *Illustrated London News*, 6th September 1856, as part of a series on the watering places of England.

© Paul Chrystal, 2023
First published in the United Kingdom, 2023,
by Stenlake Publishing Ltd.
www.stenlake.co.uk
ISBN 978-1-84033-961-1

The publishers regret that they cannot supply copies of any pictures featured in this book.

Printed by
P2D Books, 1 Newlands Rd, Westoning, Bedford MK45 5LD

BY THE SAME AUTHOR:

- Old Knaresbrough
- Old Skipton
- Old Sheffield
- Old Hartlepool & West Hartlepool
- Old Middlesborough
- Old Hessle
- Old Bradford

2—Here goes!
DRINKING THE WATERS AT HARROGATE.

Introduction

Harrogate is, by any measure, a fine and elegant town. The buildings stand as testimony of its heritage as a leading European spa town, its grand hotels, the abundance of flowers every spring, the magnificent Stray, the equally magnificent Valley Gardens, institutions like Bettys and Ogden's – all of these combine to produce a place which exudes style and breathes history, a place where it is simply good to be. Not that this has made it superior or arrogant in any way – far from it, the town has always enjoyed a reputation for being decidedly more workmanlike and informal than other spa towns such as Bath or Cheltenham.

A 1930s guide to Harrogate summed up the place: *'the Mecca of the Ailing, the Playground of the Robust'*. That motto still holds good today and still describes well the essence of Harrogate: the people may have changed and the commerce and economy may be very different but, essentially, the town retains many of the features it boasted in its early spa-driven days. This is thanks largely to some inspired commercial foresight and visionary restoration and renovation.

In 1399 Harrogate became Crown property when the possessions of the Duchy of Lancaster merged with the English Royal Crown. Until the beginning of the 19th century it may surprise visitors to the town to learn that Harrogate was much smaller than next-door Knaresborough; at the end of the 1690s it had 57 houses compared to Knaresborough's 156. Harrogate does not appear in *Domesday* and we have to wait until 1332 before its first historical reference, as part of the roll for Knaresborough Court. The name comes from the Norse *'Here gatte'*, the road to Harlow, or to Haverah, which in turn means the road to the soldier's hill. Haverah was a royal park dating back to 1100.

Thorpe's *Early History of Harrogate* published in 1891 tells us that:

Harrogate is derived from the ancient British of Heywray–gate, i.e., Hey a forest, park, or moor–wray, a brook or stream – and gate, a road. Another fixes the derivation as Harw–gate, the road of robbers...The titles with which Harrogate has been credited are so innumerable, as to suggest imperfect orthography as their source. The name may still be found in some old established railway guides as "Harrowgate;" though the w is fast losing its hold upon the heretofore confident railway tabulators. It may not be uninteresting to state that the following, besides the above mentioned, are said to have done duty in turn: "Harloo-cum-Bylton Banks," "Harlowgate," "Harrogat," "Harry-gate," and "Harrowgait."

In the Middle Ages the waters of nearby St. Mungo's and St. Robert's were credited with miraculous powers. After the mineral springs were discovered and popularised the population exploded and was at 1,500 by 1810. Harrogate spa water contains much-coveted iron, sulphur and common salt.

There are 88 wells within just two miles of the Royal Pump Room Museum; Harrogate has been called *'The Queen of Inland Watering Places'* and *'England's Premier Spa'*. But not by the people of Bath...

When Harrogate started to emerge as a place of some consequence in the 18th and 19th centuries, like all good things it attracted some bad press; this is Tobias Smollett's baleful description of his Harrogate spa experience in *The Expedition of Humphry Clinker*: *'at night I was conducted into a dark hole on the ground floor, where the tub smoked and stunk like the pit of Acheron'*. Acheron is the river that runs through Hell. After staying in the town in 1766 Smollett describes Harrogate as *'a wild common, bare and bleak, without tree or shrub or the least signs of cultivation'*. *Thorpe's Illustrated Guide* of 1886 gives us an alarming range of conditions for which the sulphur waters provide effective therapy: *'pimples which rise with great itching, ulcerated tetters, scorbutic rash, shingles, leprosies, branny scales, scaly tetter, grog blossoms produced by intemperance.'* Charles Dickens visited the Spa Rooms to deliver some readings in 1858 and said *'Harrogate is the queerest place with the strangest people in it, leading the oddest lives of dancing, newspaper reading and tables d'hote'*.

But we'll finish where we came in: Harrogate is, and remains, by any measure, a fine and elegant town.

Orphans opening stockings at Christmas. The orphanage was founded in 1897 by Miss Catherine Gurney OBE, for the care and welfare of police force children who had lost one or both parents. The children were housed at the Northern Police Orphanage on 12 acres of land on Otley Road from 1898 until they moved to Albany Lodge, Hereford Road, Harrogate in 1955. From January 1898 when the first child, Minnie Smith from Sunderland, was taken in, until closure in 1956 due to the declining numbers of children in need, a total of 644 children had passed through the doors of St. George's.

Orphans posting letters to Father Christmas. This is how one of the children later described Christmas morning:

> instead of being awakened at 6.20am by a bell ringing, Miss Knocker, dressed as Father Christmas, would blow a horn at the top of the main staircase and when washed and dressed, bedside prayers said, both boys and girls would gather at the staircase and at a further blowing of the horn, we would run around our separate wings searching for our name tagged Christmas stockings, which the staff had hidden around the house on Christmas Eve night… After breakfast we were all sent outside to see if the Postman was calling on us…

At breakfast, on each side plate, there would be coins with little slips of paper telling us that 1/-s, 2/-s, 3/-s etc had been donated to each child by a particular Police Force. The money would be held in the office by Miss Adams, under the name of each child, to be used for special occasions'.

The orphanage that was St. George's House enjoyed a close relationship with St. Andrew's Police Convalescent Home which was nearby, especially at Christmas. The children would usually stay at St. George's over Christmas: an annual tradition was the 'Stirring of the Christmas Pudding'. One evening, Miss Knocker would invite the St. Andrew's police 'inmates' to come over to St. George's; the children, staff and men would all gather in the Senior Girls' Playroom, the fire was lit and each child would come up to the huge mixing bowl to stir the pudding mix with a large wooden spoon. If there was a policeman present from the child's Force, he would be summoned to mix the pudding with the relevant child. All of the men and children got stuck in stirring the mix and making a wish.

8th August 1956 was a bad day in Nidd Vale Terrace in Harrogate. A train left Harrogate Station for Starbeck Sheds, but the route had not been set. The locomotive went into a siding and through the buffers into a window on Nidd Vale Terrace; fortunately no one was hurt. 29th May 1961 saw another accident at Starbeck when two trains were involved in a sidelong collision resulting in derailment in which 12 passengers were injured.

A busy day at the Boating Lake, or Children's Corner, or Wading Pond, in Valley Gardens. Thirty-six springs rise within one acre of the Valley Gardens (there are 88 in the town as a whole and each one is chemically different) all pumped down to the Royal Baths. The gardens were enlarged in 1901 to what is more or less their current layout. The central part was originally called Bog Fields after the boggy area which used to be there. The metal covers with their unique numbers indicating the presence of a spring or well beneath have long been removed in the interests of the efficiencies required for grass cutting.

The Metcalfe haulage contractors van all done up for the Children's Fancy Dress Ball in aid of Harrogate Infirmary. The district boasted six hospitals at one time, with facilities in Ripon, Knaresborough, Scotton and three in Harrogate town; the Royal Bath Hospital had been the Northern centre for Rheumatology diseases, Scotton Banks was originally a TB unit, Knaresborough Hospital had been the old 'poor house'. Before the current District Hospital was built in the 1970s, Harrogate was served by the General Hospital off Knaresborough Road, built in 1932. In 1883, a new purpose-built hospital was constructed on Belford Road, where St. Peter's Primary School now stands, and created 20 beds for the area at a cost of £6,250; by the turn of the 20th century, the Belford Road site was renamed the Harrogate Infirmary. The Royal Bath Hospital closed soon after the NHS stopped prescribing spa days for patients; the hospitals in Knaresborough and Scotton followed suit.

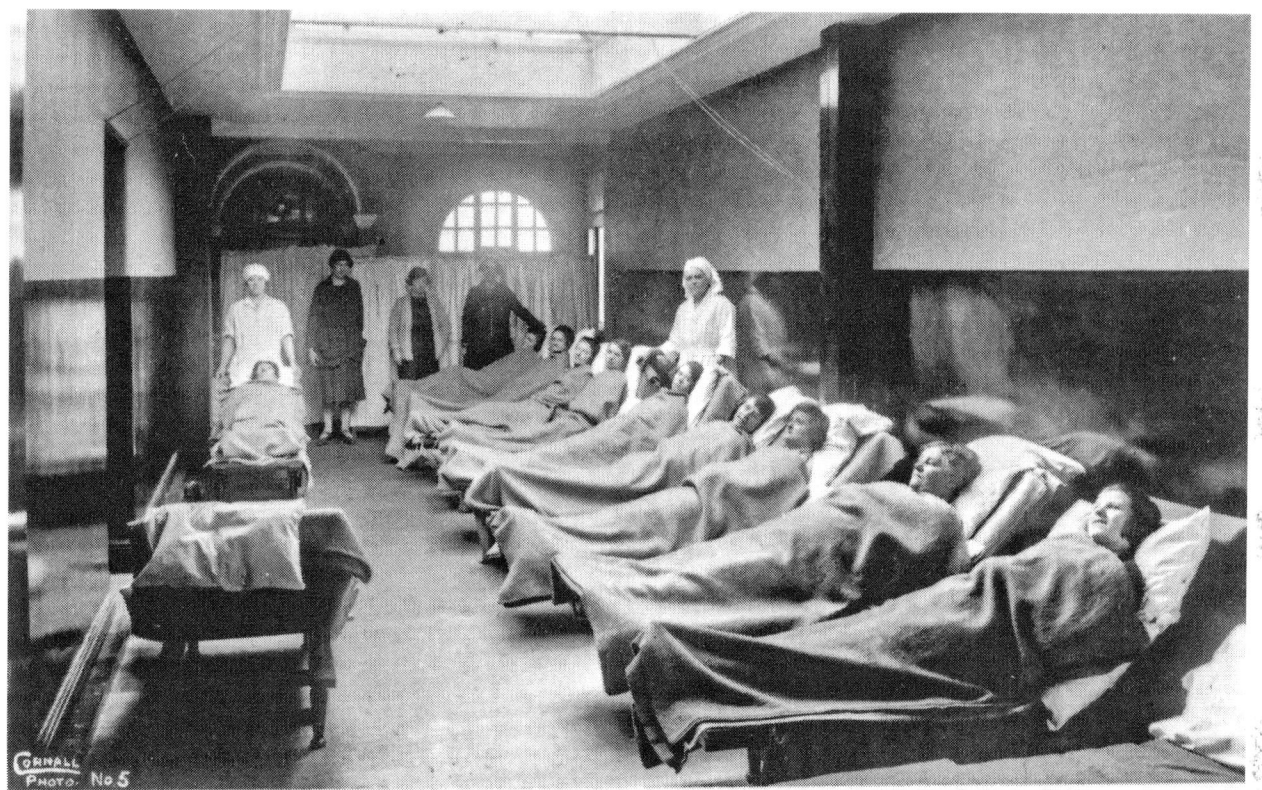

ROYAL BATH HOSPITAL & RAWSON CONVALESCENT HOME. HARROGATE.

Built by Baggalay and Bristowe in 1897 on the site of Oddy's 1819 Saline Chalybeate Pump Room, the magnificent Royal Baths opened on July 3rd 1897 and went on to provide some of the most advanced hydrotherapy treatments in the world. The baths gained a new wing in 1898 for the Peat and Plombières Baths – the latter for the very popular Plombières Two-way System or Harrogate Intestinal Lavage System – a colonic irrigation treatment which could result in the loss of half a stone in weight. They were extended in 1909 and 1911 and again in 1939 to include a new treatment wing, panelled lounge hall and the open-air fountain court. Used by the National Health Service from the late 1940s until 1968 they were then given over to private patients for a short period. By 1969 only the Turkish Sauna suite was in operation but it remains one of the most beautiful of England's last remaining Victorian baths. The 1911 extension was built to house the Plombières Baths specialising in the treatment of muco-colitis and other gastrointestinal disorders as championed by Sir Frederic Treves, Serjeant Surgeon to Edward VII. Treves carried out the first successful appendectomy in England in 1888 (until then appendicitis carried a high mortality rate) and it was he who befriended Joseph Merrick, The Elephant Man in the London Hospital for four years. With tragic irony, Treves died of peritonitis; Thomas Hardy, a close friend, composed a poem in his honour and recited it at his funeral.

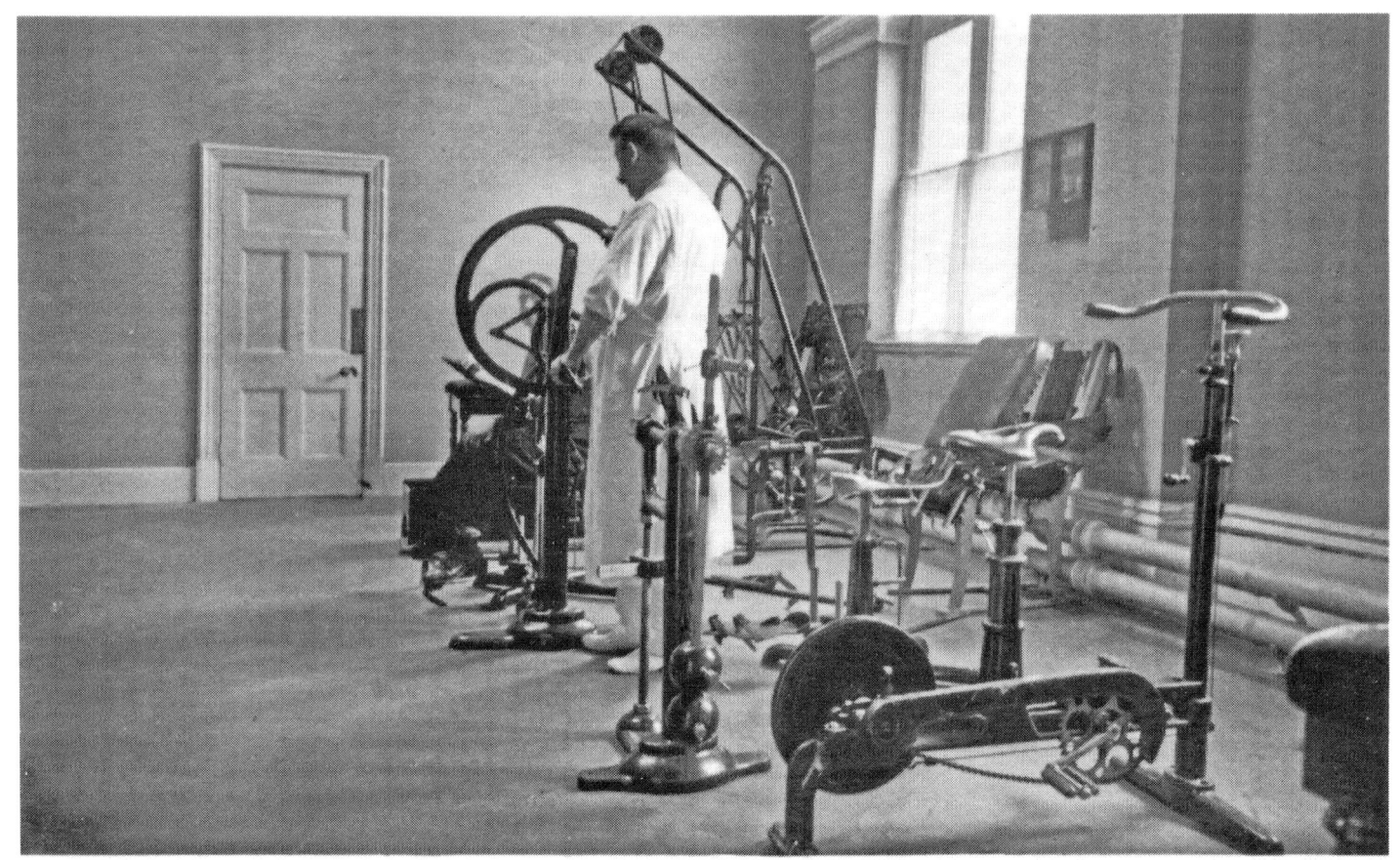

HARROGATE ROYAL BATHS.
A Corner of the Mechano-Therepeutic Dept.

The Royal Baths, built on the site of the Kissingen Well, offered around 90 different treatments catering for a wide range of disorders and diseases – real and otherwise. For many of these treatments Harrogate and the Royal Baths in particular became a centre of excellence with an international reputation. Perhaps the most famous was the Saline Sulphur Bath which comprised two waters: Saline Sulphur and Alkaline Sulphur Water, the latter used in the treatment of skin disorders, the former for gout, rheumatism and liver disease. The Nasal Douche and Throat Sprays involved using a medical device which enabled the patient to inhale atomised mineral water to remove mucous attached to the inside of the nose thus, apparently, helping with normal circulation and secretions. The beautiful fountain is now in the Royal Pump Museum.

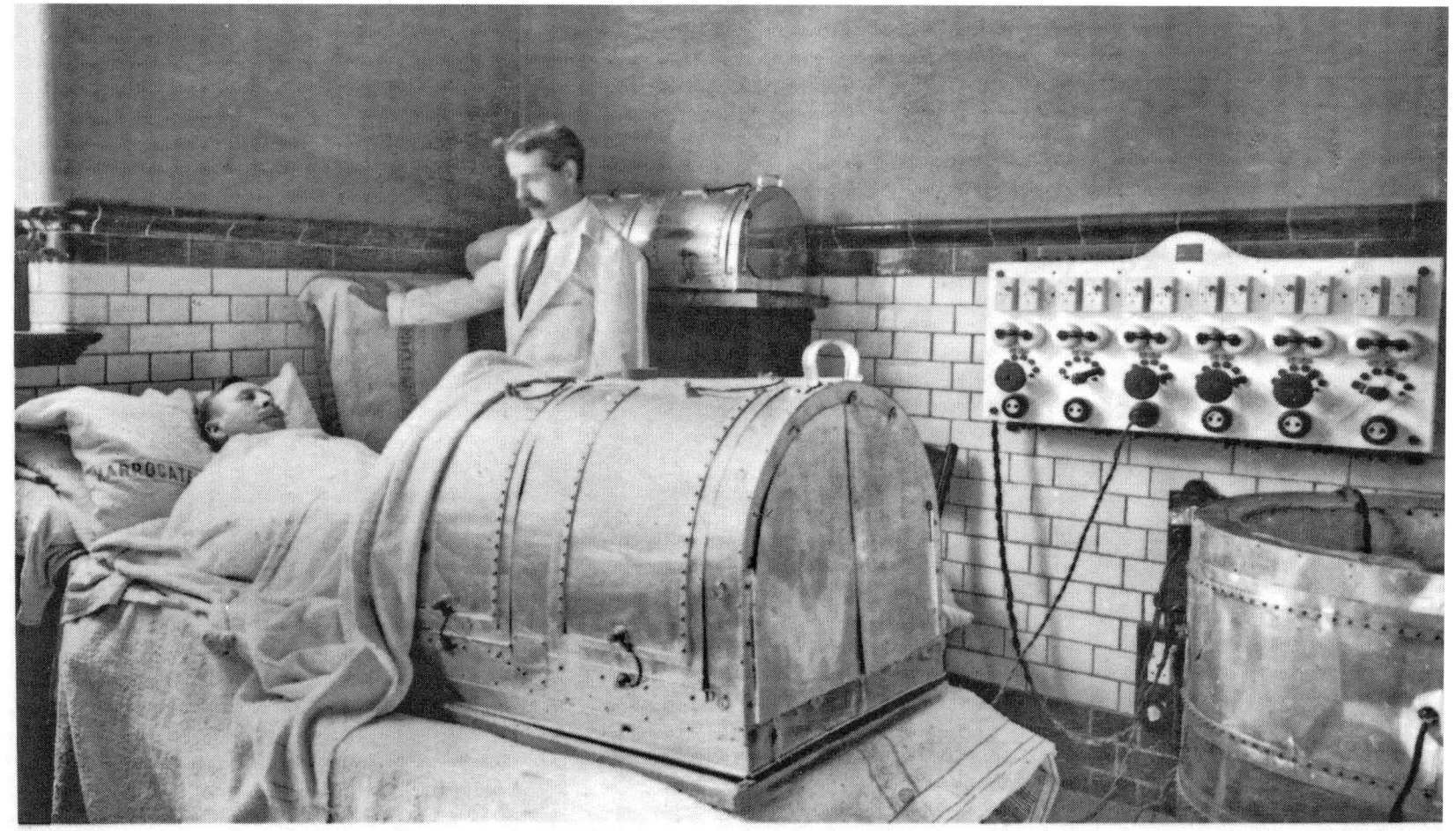

HARROGATE ROYAL BATHS.

The Royal Baths Voltaic Cage Bath emitted pulses of electricity effective in the treatment of patients with polio and MS. The uniform of the female attendants was a long bottle-green skirt, white blouse, large apron and a cap. Men wore a collar and tie and a jacket, which, in the temperatures involved, must have been insufferable. The laconium was heated to 79 degrees Fahrenheit and the caldarium a cool, by comparison, 55 degrees. One of the attendant's crucial jobs was to wipe the brows of clients lest the steaming water scalded their eyes. There were 20 women attendants and three men: because women were unable to undress themselves (the buttons on their dresses being at the back) each lady needed their own attendant.

Senior staff around 1910 on the staircase of the Winter Gardens; the orchestra is there too. The postcard boasts that treatments for muco-membranous colitis, chronic appendicitis &c are available. Peat baths were also very popular in the Royal Baths – there were four of them: Mineral Peat Bath; The Brine Bath; The Electric Bath; and the Ordinary Peat Bath. The minerals for these were brought in from the North York Moors. The baths themselves were made of Burma teak and took one week to make. Peat baths were efficacious in cases of rheumatism, lumbago, sciatica and the like.

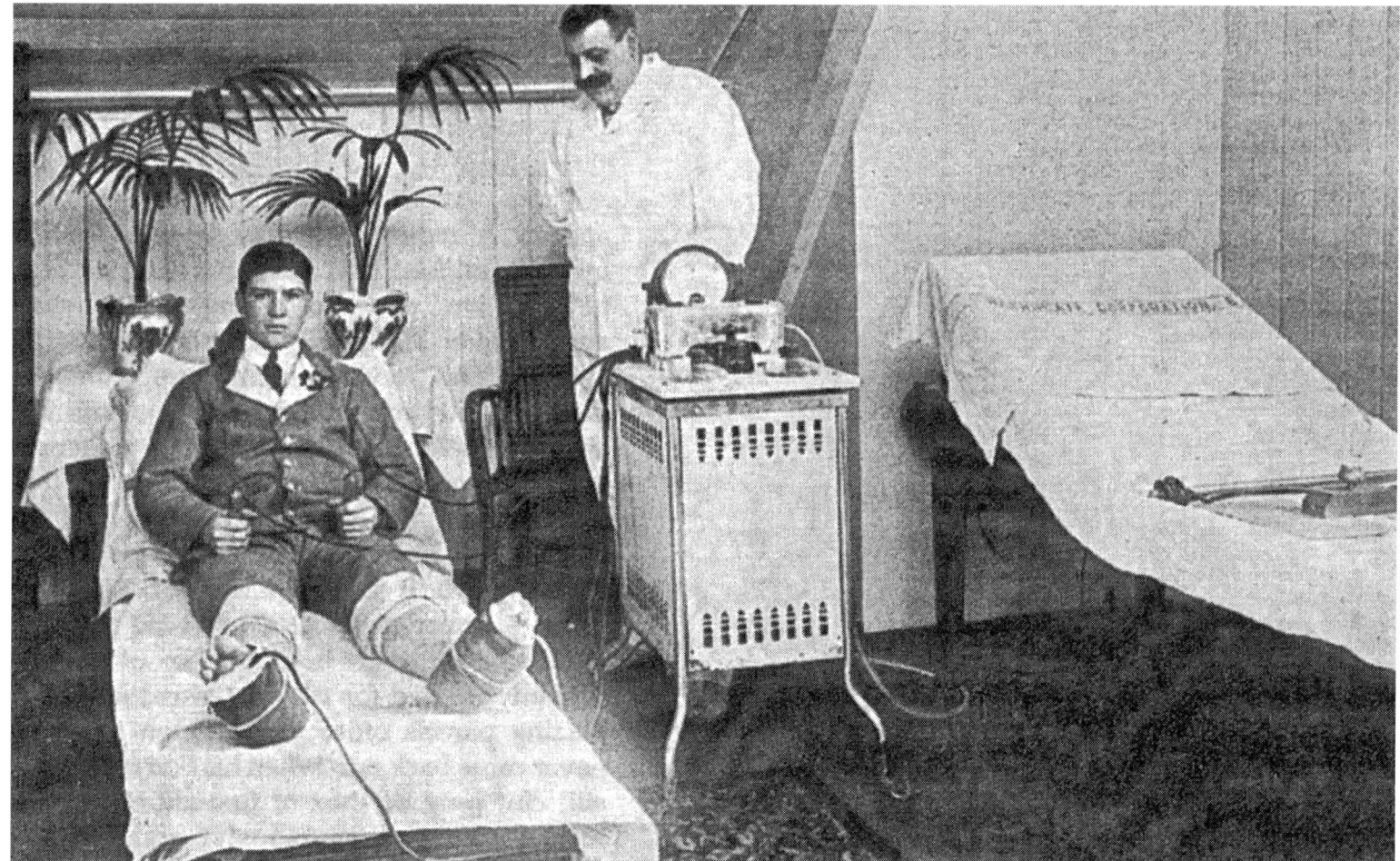

During the First World War Harrogate took on a truly patriotic, military support role when it opened its hitherto exclusive and elite doors to wounded servicemen for physical rehabilitation and mental and physical recuperation. A prodigious 100,000 servicemen were treated in 1919 alone (no separate records exist for before that) with 600 injured passing through the various doors each week. The image shows just one casualty at the Royal Bath Hospital. Harrogate, of course, benefitted: it won a reputation for being a centre of excellence for post traumatic injury assessment and rehabilitation, and it attracted business after the war which otherwise would have gone to Baden Baden in Germany, and Spa in Belgium. Unlike Wells, Bath and Buxton, Harrogate made a profit during the war.

The aftermath of the Market Hall Fire, 21st March 1914. The fire broke out on Saturday night shortly after the market inspector had made his last rounds checking the building at 11 o'clock. The town's fire station adjoined the market hall and at 11.30 one of the firemen noticed the glow of the fire within. He raised the alarm and the rest of the brigade were quickly on the scene. However, in spite of their efforts *'the fire had obtained a good hold and stall after stall became involved with remarkable rapidity'*. An estimated £10,000 worth of damage resulted.

Confectionery was big business in Harrogate, and still is. Not only did Bettys make their own chocolates as well as many other delightful confections such as Fat Rascals, but Farrah's too were turning out toffees by the van load. Founded in 1840 by John Farrah the shop was originally on Royal Parade, but closed in the mid 1990s and now stands on Montpellier Parade. The aim of their signature toffee, Original Harrogate Toffee, was to cleanse the palate of the putrid taste of Harrogate's sulphur water. Original Harrogate Toffee is similar to both butterscotch and barley sugar and uses butter, lemon and three different types of sugar to give a unique texture and flavour. It is still made in copper pans and packaged in the recognisable trade mark blue and silver embossed tins.

The Queen Victoria Jubilee Monument, in Station Square, was erected in 1887 by Mayor Richard Ellis to mark the Queen's Golden Jubilee. This was all part of the Victoria Park Company scheme to develop a new town centre linking the two Harrogates with residential and retail streets. The railway arrived in Harrogate in 1848; the new station opened in 1862 bringing trainloads of tourists and thus heralding the start of Harrogate's tourist industry. Not everyone was enthusiastic though: it was thought by some that the trains would bring the 'lower orders' to the town and reduce the milk yield from local cows.

In 1893 James Roberts Ogden opened The Little Diamond Shop in Cambridge Street, the genesis of what was to become one of Britain's most famous and prestigious jewellers. The impressive Edwardian shop front and showrooms in the current James Street shop bought in 1910 still retain many of the original Edwardian features. Down the years Ogden's has supplied jewellery and silverware to royalty and heads of state including Eleanor Roosevelt, King George VI and Princess Marina. Sir Winston Churchill had a silver cigar case made by Ogden's. J.R. Ogden was a celebrated Egyptologist and was adviser to Howard Carter and Sir Leonard Wooley. Carter of course went on to discover the tomb of Tutankhamun in 1922. Ogden was also Advising Goldsmith to the British Museum and was involved in the restoration of some of the most precious gold artefacts found in museums around the world. The company is currently run by the fourth and fifth generations of the family. Ogden's were frequently called upon to take selections of jewellery to guests in their hotels for them to choose their purchases in comfort and privacy. It is this which led to the practice of hotels having jewellery display boxes in their public areas.

Harrogate has always supported a large number of bands – they were a key part of the entertainment on offer for all those spa visitors, and the Postmen's Band was just one. Here are some key dates in the life of the Postmen's Band:

March 1915 – Harrogate Borough Band and Harrogate Postmen's Band booked to play in Valley Gardens on Sundays throughout the season.
May 1915 – Postmen's Band withdrew from Sunday performances until members are not engaged on military service.
October 1915 – Trooper H. Watson, Yorks Hussars, conductor of Harrogate Postmen's Band, is with the B.E.F. in Belgium.
April 1917 – Celebrating his golden wedding, A.W. Carrick was a bandmaster of the Harrogate Borough Band and Harrogate Postmen's Band until he left in 1919 to join the Milnsbridge Socialist Band.

Another band was Harrogate Temperance Prize Band with their headquarters in Cambridge Street opposite St. Peter's Church. In May 1917 Private A.E. Hart, Harrogate Temperance Band member for 20 years, died on his way home on leave from the front. By the early 1930s the band had changed its name to the Harrogate Silver Prize Band when temperance went out of fashion, and then to Harrogate St. John Ambulance Band during the Second World War, reverting to its Silver Band name in 1947. It disbanded in 1956.

One of their contemporaries was Harrogate Borough Band – Harrogate's second brass band which existed from the around 1900 until it disbanded at the outbreak of the Second World War. In September 1915 Ernest Abrams, former cornet player in the Borough Band, was killed by a German sniper. Other bands include the Harrogate Brass Band, Harrogate Rifle Volunteers Band; Harrogate Rifle Band and Harrogate Subscription Band to name a few.

BLACKBURN MONOPLANE ON HARROGATE STRAY 1914

Harrogate's Stray was a popular venue for air races at the dawn of aviation. Only seven years after the Wright Brothers' inaugural flight the Royal Aero Club staged a competition for the fastest plane to make the journey from London to Manchester, with a £10,000 prize. In 1911 a 'Circuit of Britain' air race starting and ending at the Brooklands racetrack near Weybridge, but taking in the whole of the country in a great loop as far north as Edinburgh took place. This was the to become the Daily Mail Air Race. Thirty aircraft initially signed up the race – though several withdrew or crashed before the start. Those which did take part included two Yorkshire-built Blackburn Mercury II monoplanes (which would have been built in Leeds, because Blackburn didn't move his factory to Brough until 1916); several Bleriot XIs; five Bristol Type T biplanes; and an Avro Type D biplane which crashed before the start. Competitors were expected to land at various points along the way. Stage 2 was from Hendon to Edinburgh (343 air miles) with two compulsory stops en route – the first of these on The Stray. Brian Catchpole in his *Balloons to Buccaneers: Yorkshire's Role in Aviation Since 1785*, tells how some 70,000 people paid between sixpence and five shillings to secure a place on the Stray while another 100,000 found their spots free of charge; roads into Harrogate were clogged with over one thousand motor cars packed on the Stray; a train arrived from Hull packed with aviation enthusiasts who were to witness '*some of the finest descents and ascents ever made in connection with aviation*'. Only five aircraft made it as far as Harrogate, including US aviator Samuel Franklin Cody in his 'Circuit of Britain' biplane; Cody's plane '*just missed the top of the Royal Hotel as he came in low over the trees*'.

Announcing the result in the January 1910 General Election in Harrogate. Before 1950 Harrogate was part of the Ripon constituency. The current constituency was created as 'Harrogate' and following boundary changes in 1997 the name was changed to Harrogate and Knaresborough. There were two general elections in 1910; the first in January when the Conservatives, under Edward Wood, won the seat back from the Liberals who had taken it in 1906; the second in December when Wood and the Conservatives again beat the Liberals but with a reduced majority. The Liberal government called the January election in the midst of a constitutional crisis – caused by the rejection of the People's Budget by the Conservative-dominated House of Lords – in order to get a mandate to pass the budget. It resulted in a hung parliament, with the Conservative Party led by Arthur Balfour and their Liberal Unionist allies receiving the largest number of votes, but the Liberals under H. H. Asquith winning the largest number of seats, returning two more MPs than the Conservatives. The Liberal government was still trying to pass its budget so they called an election to get a mandate for the Parliament Act 1911, which would prevent the House of Lords from permanently blocking legislation. After the Liberals, together with the Irish Nationalists and Labour, retained their Commons majority, the House of Lords gave way and the budget was passed.

Three businesses in Beulah Street, c. 1910, left to right: the Butter Company specialising in butter and margarine, Edwin H. Pearson, photographers at the Beulah Studio; and the Beulah Hotel.

A Shaftoe postcard showing the Bilton motor bus outside Walker Road Post Office. Walker Road is now King's Road and is home to Ascot House Hotel which trades still. A Mr W.H. Baxter (1849-1936) bought the land on which the hotel stands from Baroness de Ferrieres on 31st January 1889. Baxter ran a road-building equipment firm in Leeds. His fortune came mainly from a patent he owned on a 'Knapping Machine', used to break stones to make hardcore for roads. He owned the first electric car in Harrogate and was probably one of the earliest commuters to Leeds. Baxter was a philanthropist too, for example paying for the floodlighting of St. Luke's and donating to Harrogate Boys' Club.

Two views of the famous Pump Room/ Sulphur Wells – one from 1928, the other from the '40s or '50s. The Royal Pump Room dates from 1842 and was built under the auspices of the newly-formed Improvement Commissioners who were empowered to provide a suitable building to house the Sulphur Well – the world's strongest sulphur well; the original cover was moved to the Tewit Well where it survives today. The Pump Room was designed by Isaac Shutt and cost £3,000. Stanhope was the first to differentiate between the clientele at the different wells, describing those here as *'the vulgar sort'* and questioned the standards of hygiene when *'it was open for the promiscuous of all sorts...so that the poor Lazar* [the leprous] *impotent people do dayly environ it, whose putrid rags lie scattered...it is to be doubted whether they do wash their soares and cleanse their besmirched clouts, though unseen, where diverse persons after dippe their cups and drinke.'*

It seems that leprosy patients were tolerated when the well was open plan, but when it became closed in they were ostracised.

Celia Fiennes, the first woman to visit every county in England, came to Harrogate on her grand tour– a journey she made on horseback and frequently accompanied by only one or two servants. This is how she described the Old Sulphur Well in her *Great Journey to Newcastle and to Cornwall* in 1698:

> there is the Sulpher or Stincking spaw, not Improperly term'd for the Smell being so very strong and offensive that I could not force my horse Near the Well... the taste and smell is much of Sulpher' tho' it has an additionall offenciveness Like Carrion.

Despite this, numbers of drinkers continued to rise from 3,774 in 1842, 11,626 in 1867 and, in 1925, 259,000. The author of the 1813 *Guide to All the Watering and Sea-Bathing Places* was less than complimentary:

> Harrowgate water tastes like rotten eggs and gunpowder; and though it is probable that no person ever made a trial of such a mixture, the idea it conveys is not inapplicable ... While some places are visited because they are fashionable, and others on account of the beauty of their scenery, Harrowgate possesses neither of those attractions in a superior degree, and therefore is chiefly resorted to by the valetudinary, who frequently quaff health from its springs, else we cannot suppose that upwards of two thousand persons annually visit this sequestered spot ... it lies ... on a dreary common.

How things were to change ...

Deaf and dumb people having a taste of sulphur at the Pump Room in a Harrogate noted for its largely snobbish clientele anxious to be seen around the town and for its cultural and social one-upmanship. William Slingsby's discovery of the strange rusty looking waters of the Iron Spring, or Tuewhit, later Tewit, Well in 1571 marked the genesis of Harrogate as a world famous spa town. Dr Edmund Deane, a prominent York physician in his 1626 work *Spadacrene Anglica,* or *The English Spaw Fountaine*, tells us that Slingsby brought the new found asset to the attention of Queen Elizabeth's physician, Dr Timothy Bright. Bright, on drinking the water, *'found it in all things to agree with those at the Spaw'* – namely, the two famous medicinal springs of Sauveniere and Pouhon at Spa in Belgium's Ardennes – which happened at the time to be a den of Catholicism which the English Crown was trying to deter its subjects from visiting. Finding a spa in Harrogate (the first English town to be thus named) was literally a godsend, and from then on Harrogate's reputation was assured. Another link, albeit tenuous, between Spa and Harrogate is that Swan Hotel refugee Agatha Christie's fictional detective Hercule Poirot was born in Spa. The Well inherited the 1808 Tuscan columned temple originally at the Royal Pump Room and designed by Thomas Chippendale; it was closed in 1971 – 400 years after its opening.

A bad day for the allies which in Harrogate was conveyed by this horse-drawn news stand. The naval operations in the Dardanelles campaign (17 February 1915 – 9 January 1916) were fought against the Ottoman Empire when ships of the Royal Navy, French Marine Nationale, Imperial Russian Navy and the Royal Australian Navy, battled to take the defences of the Dardanelles Straits, a narrow, 41 mile long waterway connecting the Mediterranean Sea with the Sea of Marmara and further north to the Black Sea. Allied naval operations required the transportation of thousands of soldiers to and from the Dardanelles over the Mediterranean Sea under constant threat from attacks by German and Austrian-Hungarian submarines and mines. The worst loss during the campaign was the sinking of HMT *Royal Edward* on 13 August 1915. The ship had sailed from Alexandria to Gallipoli with 1,367 officers and men on board and was torpedoed by SM *UB-14* near the Dodecanese, with 935 lives lost.

Survivors of the *Royal Edward* in hospital gowns on board the hospital ship *Soudan*. Creative Commons Attribution-Share Alike 4.0 International licence (Ndovu09).

The Kovno (Kaunas) Forts referred to on the right hand poster proclaims the capitulation of the nine fort Kaunas Fortress in Lithuania constructed between 1882 and 1915 to protect the Russian Empire's western borders. Germany attacked the Russian Empire in August 1915 when the fortress held out for eleven days before capture. During the Second World War, parts of the fortress complex were used by Nazi Germany for detention, interrogation, and execution. About 50,000 people were executed there, including more than 30,000 victims of the Holocaust.

The White Hart Hospital, later hotel, with the Crown Hotel in the background. Built in 1846 this neo-classical building is, in Pevsner's estimation, *'easily the best building in Harrogate... with nothing gaudy or showy about it'*. The *York Courant* of 20 August 1765 is the earliest known reference to the White Hart, and announces that *'Stray'd or conveyed on the 14th August from Thomas Wray's at the White Hart in Low Harrogate, a dappled grey mare ... whoever shall give notice of the same ... 15 shillings reward and reasonable charges'*. Then it was an inn, accommodating visitors to the sulphur wells that made Harrogate England's first spa town, and the cold well at the base of what is now Cold Bath Road. It was an important stop on the coaching routes which linked Harrogate to the rest of the country. The Jarrow Crusaders paused here on the Stray to the front of the hotel in 1936 en route to London. Aneurin Bevan visited Harrogate as Minister of Health, which was earmarked to become the British Empire's principal centre for rheumatism research and treatment, and inspected the White Hart, leading to the recommendation that it, along with the neighbouring Crown Hotel, be purchased by the state to become annexe hospitals for the Royal Baths. But this was too ambitious a plan and in 1949, the White Hart passed into the hands of the Leeds Regional Hospital Board. The White Hart served as the National Health Service's only conference venue, catering to all the areas of the NHS until it was acquired by the University of York in 1988.

Burgess' Livery Stables provided the service here at White Hart Mews. Another carriage company was Mackay & Fowler Carriage Manufactory who were prominent at the end of the 19th century and specialised in Landaus fitted with Patent Automatic Head. After the First World War Harrogate witnessed a significant change in its clientele. The exclusive, aristocratic visitors of the pre-war period gave way to what was dismissively called the 'charabanc trade' – obviously not so wealthy but well enough heeled all the same. To cater for this new market the Valley Gardens were developed with the Sun Colonnade and Pavilion, and the Royal Baths were extended.

Built originally in 1740 by Joseph Thackwray, great uncle of the owner of Montpellier Square and Gardens, the Crown was renovated in 1847 and again in 1870. Thackwray was given permission to buy the Crown Hotel by King George III in 1778. In 1784 the head waiter, William Thackwray was making so much money that he was able to buy the Queen Hotel. Thackwray was no fool: in 1822 he discovered a number of new wells, one of which was a sulphur well called the Crown Well and another he channelled into the back yard of the Crown. This led to an Act of Parliament giving Harrogate powers to protect their mineral waters against such piracy.

Lord Byron stayed in 1806 with *'a string of horses, dogs and mistresses'*. Whilst here he composed *To a Beautiful Quaker*, inspired it seems when he happened to notice a pretty Quaker girl nearby. The first stanza of the poem is taken from the first edition of *Fugitive Pieces* published in 1806:

> Sweet girl! though only once we met,
> That meeting I shall ne'er forget;
> And though we ne'er may meet again,
> Remembrance will thy form retain.
> I would not say, "I love," but still
> My senses struggle with my will:
> In vain, to drive thee from my breast,
> My thoughts are more and more repress;
> In vain I check the rising sighs,
> Another to the last replies:
> Perhaps this is not love, but yet
> Our meeting I can ne'er forget.

Elgar visited in 1912. In the Second World War the Government requisitioned the Crown for the Air Ministry – they finally vacated in 1959.

Montpellier water servers in the late 19th century. Established in 1835 by Joseph Thackwray who also owned Montpellier Gardens and the Crown Hotel, 6,000 baths were taken here in the 1839 season and for many years Montpellier were considered the best baths in town; they specialised in needle shower and douche baths and invalid Sitz baths. Six new wells, including the famous Kissingen Well, were discovered when the foundations were being dug for the Montpellier Public Baths, no doubt to the delight of Thackwray. The small octagonal building, which survives, was originally a gatehouse and ticket office for the hotel's gardens.

The Majestic's origins lie in a dispute between a local businessman, Sir Blundell Maple, and the Queen Hotel. On checking his bill one morning at The Queen, Sir Blundell spotted an error; not receiving satisfaction from the Queen's manager he stormed out threatening to build a hotel which would put The Queen out of business. And so was born the Majestic: fine hotel as it was and is, it nevertheless failed to ruin The Queen. Guests have included Elgar, Winston Churchill, Errol Flynn and George Bernard Shaw. Thomas Baskerville (d. 1840) surgeon and botanist speaks plainly of his irritation at the over-eager water servants invading even The Queen's hotel rooms to ladle out the water: guests were met with '"I am pretty Betty, let me serve you"..."Kate and Cozen Doll, do let we tend you..." but to tell the truth they fell short of that for their faces shone like bacon rine. And for beauty may view with an old Bath guide's ass.'

The hotel was badly damaged by fire in 1924 causing £50,000 worth of damage. It also has the dubious distinction of being on the wrong end of one of three bombs Harrogate received during the Second World War. The hotel was listed as a target for German bombers in 1940 because German intelligence wrongly had it down as the headquarters of the Air Ministry. Indeed, Harrogate was second in the list of priority targets which includes Hughendon Manor at the top (headquarters of Fighter Command); various garrisons, the headquarters of Bomber Command, the Admiralty and other sensitive installations. In the event a Junkers 88 dropped three bombs at midday on September 12th 1940: one exploded in the hotel gardens, one on the corner of Swan and Ripon Roads demolishing a house, and the other hit The Majestic but failed to explode. This was rendered safe by a Captain G.H. Yates of the bomb disposal squad.

A concert in full swing in the Winter Gardens in the 1920s, possibly Cecil Moon's Palm Court Trio. Popular it certainly was with standing room only; however, not everyone was transfixed: take a look at the two ladies and gentleman at the front on the left ensconced in their newspapers and book; likewise those on the right behind the pianist. The Gardens were opened in 1897 and demolished in 1936 when the Lounge Hall and Fountain Court were built to replace them. All that remains are the original stone entrance foyer and staircase. Today Wetherspoons runs the establishment, but the days of such top class entertainment by the likes of Britten, Segovia, du Pré, and Menuhin are over.

This photograph from 1903 shows Otto Schwartz and his seven piece band playing one of their frequent concerts outside the Prospect Hotel. Schwartz is the one on the left playing the flute. Entertainment of a different sort came in the composition of verses on the town and its visitors; one example describes a Benjamin Blunderhead: *'And that night for the first time I stagger'd to bed,/ With more wine on my stomach than sense in my head,/ But a dose of the water as soon as t'was day,/ Dispers'd all my headache and left me quite gay.'*

Modelled loosely on the resplendent Ostende Kursaal, in Belgium (*inset*), Harrogate's Kursaal was opened in May 1903 by Sir Hubert Parry (of *Jerusalem* and *I Was Glad* fame) on the site of Bown's 1870 Cheltenham Pump Room. Early attractions included Sarah Bernhardt, the Hallé Orchestra, Anne Pavlova and Dame Nellie Melba. The name Kursaal (Cure Hall) comes from the buildings so-named and popular in continental spa towns; in Harrogate the name was changed in 1918 to the less Germanic Royal Hall and boasted 1,276 seats. The Kursaal came about as a response to the growing demand for entertainment in Harrogate and, because, at the time, the popularity of Chloride of Water was declining, the Cheltenham Pump Room was demolished to make way for it.

The Great Yorkshire Show came to be in October 1837 when a group of leading agriculturalists, led by the third Earl Spencer, met at the Black Swan Hotel in Coney Street, York to discuss the future of the farming industry. The result was the inauguration of the Yorkshire Agricultural Society – whose aims were to improve and develop agriculture and to hold a prestigious annual show. The first Yorkshire Show was held in Fulford, York, in 1838. The first recorded attendance figures were in 1842 when the Show was again held in York attracting 6,044 visitors. Before 1951 when Harrogate became the official home, the Great Yorkshire Show was held in a different town every year. Now, the three day event attracts over 100,000 visitors onto its 350 acre site and becomes the temporary home for 8,000 animals, including 1,000 horses and ponies. Over 900 stalls and stands offer every kind of product and service imaginable. Competition classes ranged across 24 different sections with 12,000 entrants, from driving four in hand coaches, to classes for honey, poultry, show jumping and the cattle, sheep and pigs. For example, the Cock o' the North Championship involves about 2,000 horses and ponies competing over three days. Polienta Co of Reading are manufacturers of cod liver oil preparations for cattle and other animals. Their leading patented product is Codelettes.

Shaftoe's and Mrs Shafoe – newsagent and tobacconist at 12 King's Road with a window full of postcards for sale. H. Shaftoe was a prominent publisher and printer of postcards with examples of their work still appearing on line today. The first known picture postcard was sent in 1840 by Theodore Hook to himself in Fulham. A writer and practical joker noted for his pranks, Hook probably sent the card as a joke since its illustration caricatures postal workers; in 2002 this card was bought for £31,750. It wasn't until 1894 that the Royal Mail allowed mass-produced picture postcards to be sent. As you might expect, most postcards were made from card – but others made of wood, copper, silk and coconut are known. The collecting of postcards became known, soon became all the rage and is now the world's fourth largest collecting hobby after stamps and coins and banknotes. We have the French to thank for the early rise of postcard production: the opening of the Eiffel Tower in 1889 boosted the dissemination of the postcard, giving rise to the 'golden age' of the picture postcard from 1898-1919, largely photochromes produced from black and white photographs. Whole sections of shops were given over to stocks of postcards in Edwardian days.

Mrs. Brogden's Wool Slipper Stand which was beyond the Magnesia Well Cafe near Valley Drive – the 1880s equivalent of a pop-up shop? The wool business continued in Harrogate for a while with Westmorland Sheepskins which traded from 1981-2022 in the town, on Montpellier Parade. Their warehouse remains in nearby Poole-in-Wharfedale – the company is still very much alive, online and visiting trade fairs and markets countrywide. As with Mrs Brogden, Westmorland specialised in woolen slippers. Westmorland Sheepskins was the off-shoot of the family business 'Heatons' which sold all things sheepskin for over 130 years in Leeds. Mrs Brogden and Westmorland Sheepskins benefitted from being on the edge of Yorkshire's textile industry.

Dickinson's the grocer was next door to Buckley's the drapers: they became one around 1900, on the corner of Chapel and Parliament Streets.

The Enterprise – a jack of all trades in Skipton Road about 1900: photographic studio, ice creams and hot peas on the left.

Staff from Harrogate, Starbeck, Leeds and Bradford congregating outside the original Bettys in Harrogate just before the 1931 outing to Windermere. Five charabancs carried the 120 or so staff over to the Lake District. Owner Frederick Belmont can be seen at the front in the middle. The story of Bettys begins in September 1907 when a twenty-two year old Fritz Butzer arrived in England from Switzerland with no English and less of any idea of how to reach a town that sounded vaguely like 'Bratwurst', where a job awaited him. Fritz eventually landed up in Bradford and found work with a Swiss confectioners called Bonnet & Sons at 44 Darley Street – whether Bradford was the original objective and whether Bonnet's was the intended employer is doubtful – who paid him the equivalent of 120 Swiss francs per month with free board. Cashing in on the fashionability of all things French Fritz changed his name to Frederick Belmont.

Courtesy of Bettys & Taylors.

Tea testing at Taylor's by veteran tea-taster and Taylor's last chairman, James Raleigh (1907-1999). Courtesy of Bettys & Taylors. The famous Tea House, run by Taylors, was in Valley Gardens. Taylors also handled the catering at the Winter Gardens and at the Royal Spa Concert Rooms.

Taylors of Harrogate has its origins during the reign of Victoria when in 1886, Quaker Charles Edward Taylor and his brother Llewellyn – sons of a York pea-dealer and master grocer – set up the tea and coffee importing business C.E. Taylor & Co. Both brothers were apprenticed at the famous Ashby's Tea of London, where they also went on to buy their teas and coffees at auction. Llewellyn eventually took a back seat but Charles opened up 'kiosk' tea and coffee tasting rooms in the popular, fashionable spa towns of Harrogate (at 11 Parliament Street) and Ilkley. The kiosks were followed by Cafe Imperials in both towns: Ilkley opened in 1896; the Harrogate branch in 1905 in the mock Scottish castle now occupied by Bettys. The Ilkley Bettys is the old Taylors 'Kiosk' Cafe and Bettys in York's Stonegate (now closed) occupied the former Taylors 'Kiosk' cafe.

New College was an independent preparatory school which amalgamated with Ashville College in 1930. It was founded as Turton Hall School in 1850 and transferred from Gildersome, south of Leeds, to Harrogate in 1898. The Rev John Haslam DD was Proprietor of Turton Hall School from 1873 and when the lease ran out in 1898 he purchased land and built New College in Harrogate for £10,000. In 1900 the New College estate comprised 34 acres and included a vegetable garden, a farm, two fives courts; a gymnasium; a workshop, two tennis courts, a cinder court and a bicycle track. The Boys' Department comprised a large dining hall and assembly room with a raised platform for choir and organ for Divine Service, three class rooms, a school parlour, a library, a music room, laboratory, a bath and dressing room, lavatory, boot and two cloak rooms. The Senior Dormitory had dressing cubicles as recommended by Dr. Clement Dukes in his book on *Health at School*. 'All the rooms were heated with hot water pipes, and ventilated on the most approved principles. Special attention was given to the sanitary arrangements' After the First World War New College boomed: from 1919 to 1923 there were more than 100 boys there. Typical school trips included climbing the Matterhorn or flying to Paris, on a Handley Page aircraft, from Croydon Airport.

Harlow Carr is one of five public gardens run by the Royal Horticultural Society, acquired by the merger of the Northern Horticultural Society with the RHS in 2001. It had been the Northern Horticultural Society's trial ground and display garden since 1946 where the suitability of plants for growing in northern climates could be studied and assessed. The Society leased 10.5 hectares of mixed woodland, pasture and arable land from Harrogate Corporation and opened the Harlow Carr Botanical Gardens in 1950. Sulphur springs were discovered on the site in the 18th century but there was no development of the spa for over a hundred years. In 1840, the owner of the estate, Henry Wright, cleaned out one of the wells and four years later built a hotel and a bath house, charging 2s 6d to bathe in the warm waters. The gardens were laid out around the bath house. The hotel was the Harrogate Arms, but is now closed. The bath house now is the garden study centre. The six well heads in front of the bath house have been capped off but remain beneath the present Limestone Rock Garden. There is a Bettys here and one of the best bookshops in the north of England. There used to be a bandstand which held frequent pierrot shows. Although the Corporation had bought Harlow Moor in 1898 it could not afford the Carr so this was bought privately for £8,500 by three councillors in 1914 who thus secured the Gardens for the town. The six imposing Doric columns were salvaged from the Cheltenham Spa Rooms which were demolished in 1939.

Harrogate Pierriots, led by Thomas Henry Coleman (born London, 1867) of Harrogate. Coleman's Pierriots entertained in parks and gardens, the Stray, and the streets of Harrogate, where they played the portable piano in a converted pram pictured here; they also performed to wounded soldiers in military hospitals during the First World War. Coleman was a friend of the Tsar Nicholas II of Russia, for whom his troupe performed in Moscow. After the Harrogate Pierrots, Coleman ran a music shop in Lowther Arcade. The publisher: Mark E. (Edward) Mitchell & Co., Prospect Studio, 6 Montpellier Parade, Harrogate; went into receivership in 1932.

One of the most historic and oldest pubs in Harrogate, Hales Bar is the town's only traditionally gas-lit bar. Its origins hail as far back as the earliest days of the town's rise as a leading spa resort and it was one of the first inns to cater for spa visitors after sulphur wells were first established in the mid-17th century. Sulphur springs still bubble beneath the cellar and their unique smell occasionally percolate up to the bar area. Hales Bar took over the licence of the Promenade Inn when the latter closed in 1840 and was bought by the brewer and developer Thomas Humble Walker for £1,220. Mr Walker extended the old Promenade during the 1840s: the older building was converted into a house, the newer part became an inn which initially took the name of the new landlord, Hodgson. In about 1882, Hodgson was replaced by William Hale and the eponymous naming continued. The main saloon bar preserves the Victorian atmosphere well, with mirrors and other interesting features and fittings from Victorian days, including those traditional gas lighting and cigar lighters. Tobias Smollett possibly drank here when in May 1766 he visited Harrogate – the setting for part of his novel *The Expedition of Humphry Clinker*. Hales was a favourite too of Sir John Barbirolli when the Hallé Orchestra was in town; some interior scenes for *Chariots of Fire* were set here. There is a good display of local history books too.

The swan sign was made to commemorate the coronation of Queen Elizabeth II in 1953. The Beatles stayed here during their 1963 visit for the concert at the Royal Hall; General Manager Geoffrey Wright was appalled at the idea of them darkening his portals. The group had tried to get into the Hotel St. George, but were turned away because their appearance was deemed inappropriate.

It had not always been clean living and the high life in Harrogate: in 1821 the people of Harrogate complained to the council about sporadic vandalism: *'during the night some persons unknown…have put into the mineral springs some quantities of Dung, Ashes, Dead Dogs, and other animals of a most offensive nature.'* In 1841 the Harrogate Improvement Act was passed to protect the springs.

In 1926 Agatha Christie took refuge at the Old Swan Hotel (at which time it was the Harrogate Hydro). The following account is taken from the hotel's brochure. She had left her home in Sunningdale, Berkshire about 9.45pm on December 3rd, abandoned her car perched precariously on the edge of a chalk pit and caught a train to Harrogate after seeing a railway poster advertising the resort. She checked in under the name of Theresa Neele, the name of her husband's mistress, and set about enjoying her stay – so began the hotel's association with murder, mystery and suspense. A week's stay cost £5 10s then. Meanwhile, a nationwide search was under way – the first in the country to involve aeroplanes. After ten days Bob Tappin, a banjo player at the hotel, recognised Mrs Christie, alerted the police, and thus drew a close to this particular mystery. In 1979 *Agatha* the film was released starring Vanessa Redgrave, Dustin Hoffman and Timothy Dalton; some of which was shot in the Swan and nearby.

A Royal Air Force station at Menwith Hill providing communications and intelligence services to the UK and the USA. The site, codename MOONPENNY, contains an extensive satellite ground station and is a communications intercept and missile warning site; it is probably the largest electronic monitoring station in the world. In the 1990s British journalist Duncan Campbell and New Zealand journalist Nicky Hager alleged in *Somebody's Listening* that the US was exploiting ECHELON traffic for industrial espionage, rather than for military and diplomatic purposes. Examples alleged include the gear-less wind turbine technology designed by the German firm Enercon, and the speech technology developed by the Belgian firm Lernout & Hauspie. The NSA admit to having spied on and intercepted the phone calls of Princess Diana until her death with Dodi Fayed in 1997 and to holding 1,056 pages of classified information about the princess, which has been classified as top secret *'because their disclosure could reasonably be expected to cause exceptionally grave damage to the national security.'* During the 2009 G-20 London Summit NSA specialists based at Menwith Hill attempted to target and decode the encrypted telephone calls of the Russian president Dmitry Medvedev.